City Animals

Claire Llewellyn

W
FRANKLIN WATTS
LONDON • SYDNEY

First published in 2003
by Franklin Watts
338 Euston Road
London NW1 3BH

Franklin Watts Australia
Level 17/207 Kent Street
Sydney NSW 2000

Text copyright © Claire Llewellyn 2003
Design and concept © Franklin Watts 2003

Educational advisor: Gill Matthews, non-fiction
 literacy consultant and Inset trainer
Editor: Rachel Cooke
Designer: James Marks
Acknowledgements: Ian Beames/Ecoscene: 14. Franco/Bonnard-Bios/Still Pictures: 17. Anthony Cooper/
Ecoscene: 15. Georges Dif/Still Pictures: front cover, 18. Jeremy Early/FLPA: 13. Jamie Harron/Ecoscene: 19.
Brian Hawkes/NHPA: 6cr. David Hosking/FLPA: 7. E.A. Janes/NHPA: 10. Michael Leach/NHPA: 16. James
Marchington/Ecoscene: 11, 23l. S. Maslowski/FLPA: 5tr, 22l. Ray Moller: 15t. Robin Redfern/Ecoscene: 1, 12, 20,
23r. Roland Seitre/Still Pictures: 21. Jurgen and Christine Sohns/FLPA: 6bl. Laurent Touzeau/Still Pictures: 2, 8-9.
Terry Whitaker/FLPA: 4, 22r. David Woodfall/NHPA: 5bl.

A CIP catalogue record for this book is available from the British Library.

ISBN: 978 0 7496 8121 0

Printed in Malaysia

Franklin Watts is a division of Hachette Children's Books, an Hachette Livre UK company.

Contents

In the city

Wild animals live in cities all over the world. They find food and shelter there.

▲ *In Asia, monkeys live in the streets.*

In America, racoons find food in rubbish bins.

You see birds in every city.

What is the difference between a pet and a wild animal?

5

City birds

Many birds make their homes in cities.

They perch on statues...

and nest on buildings.

Have you ever been woken by birds singing early in the morning? This is called the dawn chorus.

They sing from the rooftops.

On the street

Many animals find food on city streets. They eat food that we throw away.

Foxes hunt through the rubbish at night.

City and country
animals face
different kinds
of danger.
Can you think
what these
dangers are?

In the park

Parks are green spaces in a city. Animals live in the flowers, trees and ponds.

Squirrels feed in the trees – and in rubbish bins.

Often, people feed the birds in parks.

Animals that live in parks are almost tame because they get used to people.

In city homes

Many small animals live in city homes.

▲ *Mice live in the walls and under the floors.*

House spiders sometimes find their way into the bath.

What sort of wild animals have you seen in your home?

In back gardens

Many animals live in city gardens.
These small green spaces are just like little parks.

▶ *Birds feed seeds and grubs to their young.*

Pet cats in city gardens are one of the biggest dangers to wild animals. Why do you think this is?

▲ Frogs lay their eggs in garden ponds.

In the churchyard

City churchyards are green and quiet. Animals live here, too.

▶ *A snail slides over a gravestone looking for food.*

An owl feeds on a mouse, a mouse feeds on seeds and grass. This is called a food chain.

Owls hunt for mice at night.

At the rubbish dump

Rubbish dumps are dirty places, but there is plenty there to eat.

Flocks of seagulls feed at the dumps.

Why do you think so many city animals find food in rubbish dumps and bins?

This bear is hunting for food in the rubbish.

All over the city!

One kind of animal lives all over the city. It is the rat!

Rats live near restaurants and on building sites.

Rats are dirty and can give people diseases. They are pests in the city.

They live under the ground.

I know that...

1 Many wild animals live in cities.

3 Many birds live in cities.

4 Some animals live on the city streets.

2 Animals find food and shelter in a city.

5 Some animals live in parks.

6 Many animals live in city homes and gardens.

7 Others live in churchyards.

8 Many animals live on rubbish dumps.

9 Rats live all over the city.

Index

About this book

I Know That! is designed to introduce children to the process of gathering information and using reference books, one of the key skills needed to begin more formal learning at school. For this reason, each book's structure reflects the information books children will use later in their learning career – with key information in the main text and additional facts and ideas in the captions. The panels give an opportunity for further activities, ideas or discussions. The contents page and index are helpful reference guides.

The language is carefully chosen to be accessible to children just beginning to read. Illustrations support the text but also give information in their own right; active consideration and discussion of images is another key referencing skill. The main aim of the series is to build confidence - showing children how much they already know and giving them the ability to gather new information for themselves. With this in mind, the *I know that...* section at the end of the book is a simple way for children to revisit what they already know as well as what they have learnt from reading the book.